SAN DIEGO

PHOTOGRAPHY BY GREG LAWSON

Published in the United States by

First Choice

P.O. Box 21291
El Cajon, California 92021

Library of Congress Catalog Number 82-071547

SAN DIEGO ISBN 0-916251-37-3 Hardcover

0-916251-38-1 Softcover
Fifth Printing

PHOTOGRAPHY / GREG LAWSON
TEXT / DAVID MICHAELS
ART DIRECTOR / RALPH CERNUDA
TRANSLATIONS /
SUZANNE LAFOND, EVELYNE BERKMULLER,
RICHARD NANCE, EIICHI YAMAMOTO
BOTANICAL CAPTIONS / MARY SHELDON
TYPOGRAPHY / FRIEDRICH TYPOGRAPHY
PRINTED IN SINGAPORE

Our titles currently available or in production include: ARIZONA, CALIFORNIA, COLORADO, HAWAII, LOS ANGELES,
OH...CALIFORNIA, PALM SPRINGS, SAN DIEGO, SAN DIEGO COUNTY, SAN FRANCISCO, SANTA BARBARA, WESTERN OREGON.

Cover: San Diego Bay

SAN DIEGO

People are drawn to San Diego. Being one of America's large and important cities it is only natural that it would host many visitors, but the San Diego area lures its visitors back again and again, many of them choosing to be permanent residents.

What is the lure of San Diego? For many it is no doubt the salutary climate which is sometimes compared to that of the Mediterranean. It is relatively low in humidity and precipitation, but high in comfortability, averaging around 70° Fahrenheit.

For those with an affinity for water there seems to be no end to the Pacific playground along the shores of San Diego County. The varied coastline offers an ideal place to fish, swim, dive, surf or sail all year long. There are clean expansive beaches and rocky coves. There is beautiful San Diego Harbor, teeming with life and multifaceted Mission Bay Park with its captivating Sea World. At the foot of downtown is the floating Maritime Museum, and nearby a unique new bayside shopping area called Seaport Village. Alluring resort communities also dot the water's edge. Few can pass up lovely La Jolla, the "Jewel of the Pacific," or the island atmosphere of Coronado.

On the historic side, Cabrillo National Monument at the tip of Point Loma commemorates the discovery of coastal California some four and one half centuries ago by Juan Rodriguez Cabrillo. Old Town State Historic Park preserves the birthplace of California and San Diego. In Old Town many of California's earliest structures are still being used as restaurants and shops, as well as museums.

South of Old Town is the modern downtown area, an ever expanding showcase of thoughtful renovation and modern design.

One of the largest city parks in the world sits adjacent to downtown San Diego. Lush Balboa Park features excellent museums, theaters and galleries with outstanding architecture reflecting the city's Spanish heritage. Here too is the famous San Diego Zoo with its wealth of exotic plants and animals. The Zoo also maintains a large wildlife sanctuary north of the city called The San Diego Wild Animal Park where you can observe many animals roaming freely as they would in their native environment.

Moving eastward from the County's shoreline through the villages, towns and cities, past commercial flower fields, farms and orchards, through colorful and productive valleys, you soon reach the backyard of the metropolitan area. This is a different world with towering mountains, fields adorned with wildflowers, lakes, intermittent rivers and wildlife. Much of this is protected by the vast Cleveland National Forest and several California State Parks.

With so much going for it, it's no mystery that the world keeps responding to the lure of San Diego.

SAN DIEGO

Avec son charme particulier, San Diego, une des grandes villes de renom d'Amérique, attire les visiteurs qui y reviennent maintes et maintes fois et s'y installent finalement, séduits par ses attraits.

Quels sont donc les attraits de San Diego? Pour un grand nombre de visiteurs, c'est le climat salutaire qui ressemble beaucoup au climat méditerranéen. La température en moyenne est de 21 degrés Centigrade. Il y a relativement très peu de pluie et l'humidité n'est pas élevée.

Ceux qui ont une affinité avec la mer, le Pacifique offre le long de la côte du County de San Diego, un endroit de récréation sans fin. Le littoral varié de cette région est idéal pour la pêche, la natation, le plongeon et l'aquaplane tout au long de l'année. Vous y trouverez des étendues de plages et de jolies baies rocheuses. Il y a aussi le beau port de San Diego fourmillant d'énergie et le parc Mission Bay avec ses nombreux divertissements, entre autre le Sea World. Dans le centre ville, le musée maritime flottant et, tout près, le charmant quartier commerçant Seaport Village. La côte est parsemée d'attrayantes stations balnéaires. La Jolla, "le Joyau du Pacifique" et Coronado avec son ambiance insulaire attirent elles aussi les visiteurs de partout.

Du point de vue historique, le Monument Cabrillo, à l'extrémité de la Pointe Loma, rappelle la découverte de la côte californienne il y a déjà quatre siècles et demi, par Juan Rodriguez Cabrillo. Old Town State Historic Park sert à commémorer le lieu d'origine de la Californie et de la ville de San Diego. Dans la vieille partie de la ville "Old Town" on préserve beaucoup d'édifices qui servent maintenant à loger des restaurants, des boutiques ainsi que quelques musées.

Au sud de Old Town, se trouve le centre ville de San Diego où l'on observe un mélange artistique du vieux et du moderne. Un des plus grands parcs du monde avoisine le centre de la ville. Le parc Balboa, entouré de végétation luxuriante, offre d'excellents musées, théatres et galeries d'art, le tout ayant une architecture hispanique propre à l'heritage espagnol de la ville de San Diego. On y trouve aussi le jardin zoologique de grande renommée avec ses plantes exotiques et ses animaux rares. En plus, au nord de la ville il y a un refuge pour bêtes sauvages présentées dans des conditions rappelant leur vie en liberté.

Allant vers l'est et passant par les villes et villages, les champs fleuris d'horticulteurs locaux, on voit les fermes, les vergers, on traverse des vallées fécondes et pittoresques et on arrive bientôt à l'arrière plan du site métropolitain. C'est un tout autre monde, les montagnes aux hautes cîmes, les champs parés de fleurs sauvages, les lacs, les rivières ruisselantes, les bêtes sauvages, tout y abonde. Le système des parcs en Californie protège et abrite ses richesses naturelles.

Est-ce ainsi surprenant que San Diego puisse si bien nous séduire?

SAN DIEGO

San Diego ist eine Stadt mit großer Anziehungskraft. Als eine von Amerikas großen und wichtigen Städten beherbergt sie natürlich zahlreiche Gäste, doch der Reiz San Diegos und seiner Umgebung läßt seine Besucher immer wiederkehren, ja viele von ihnen erwählen die Stadt sogar zu ihrem ständigen Wohnsitz.

Was macht diese Stadt so reizvoll? Zweifellos ist es für viele das bekömmliche Klima, das auch mit dem des Mittelmeeres verglichen wird. Verhältnismäßig geringe Luftfeuchtigkeit und wenig Niederschläge, bei einer Durchschnittstemperatur von 21°C, machen es besonders verträglich.

Für alle, deren Element das Wasser ist, bieten sich die Strände von San Diego und Umgebung als schier unerschöpfliche Tummelplätze an. Die mannigfaltig gestaltete Küste bietet das ganze Jahr über ideale Gelegenheiten zum Fischen, Schwimmen, Tauchen, Surfen oder Segeln. Hier findet man saubere, weitläufige Strände und felsige Buchten. Dort liegt auch der schöne Hafen von San Diego mit seiner betriebsamen Geschäftigkeit sowie der vielartige Mission Bay Park mit seiner faszinierenden Sea World. Am Rande der Innenstadt liegt das Maritime Museum, ein schwimmendes Schiffahrtsmuseum, und ganz in der Nähe, in der Bucht gelegen, das neue, ungewöhnliche Einkaufszentrum Seaport Village. Die Küste wird von bezaubernden Badeorten belebt. Es gibt kaum jemand, der das liebliche La Jolla, die "Perle des Pazifik" oder die Inselatmosphäre von Coronado nicht erleben möchte.

Geschichtlich errinnert das Cabrillo National Monument am äußeren Ende von Point Loma an die Entdeckung der kalifornischen Küste vor ungefähr viereinhalb Jahrhunderten durch Juan Rodriguez Cabrillo.

Im Old Town State Historic Park werden die Geburtsstätten Kaliforniens und San Diegos erhalten. Dort, in der Altstadt, werden viele der ältesten Gebäude Kaliforniens noch als Restaurants, Geschäfte und Museen benutzt.

Südlich der Altstadt gibt die ständig wachsende moderne Innenstadt ein Beispiel für das Harmonieren gut durchdachter Renovierung und modernem Entwurf.

San Diegos Innenstadt grenzt an einen der größten Stadtparks der Welt. Der üppig bewachsene Bilboa Park beherbergt ausgezeichnete Museen, Theater und Gallerien, deren eindrucksvolle Architektur das spanische Erbe der Stadt widerspiegelt. Hier befindet sich auch der berühmte San Diego Zoo mit seinem Reichtum an exotischen Tieren und Pflanzen. Der Zoo unterhält außerdem nördlich der Stadt ein Tierschutzgebiet, bekannt als The San Diego Wild Animal Park. Dort kann man viele Tiere in freier Wildbahn beobachten.

Verläßt man die Küste von San Diego County in östlicher Richtung, so kommt man durch Dörfer und Städte, vorbei an Blumenfeldern, Farmen und Obstplantagen durch farbenprächtige und ertragreiche Täler und erreicht bald das Hinterland der Metropole. Eine andere Welt öffnet sich hier, mit ragenden Gipfeln, Bergwiesen, Seen, Flüssen und heimischen Tieren. Der größte Teil dieser Gegend steht unter dem Naturschutz des ausgedehnten Cleveland National Forest und mehrerer California State Parks.

Bei all diesen Vorzügen ist es kein Wunder, daß in aller Welt San Diego immer wieder als ein höchst verlockendes Reiseziel betrachtet wird.

SAN DIEGO

El público se siente atraído a San Diego. Siendo ésta una de las grandes cuidades importantes de Norteamérica, es muy natural que hospede a muchos visitantes. De hecho, el área extendida de San Diego atrae de nuevo a sus visitantes para que vuelvan una y otra vez, muchos de ellos llegando a hacerse residentes permanentes.

¿Cuál es la gran atracción de San Diego? Para muchos, sin duda, es el clima saludable que se compara a veces con el del Mediterráneo. Tiene humedad y precipitación relativamente bajas, pero sobresale en comodidad, con una temperatura mediana alrededor de los 21 grados Centígrados.

Para los que sienten gran atracción por el agua, parece haber un sinfín de áreas recreativas a lo largo de las playas del Pacífico del Condado de San Diego. La costa variada ofrece el lugar ideal para pescar, nadar, bucear, para practicar tabla hawaiana o darse a la vela el año entero. Hay limpias playas extensivas y ensenadas peñascosas. Hay el hermoso Puerto de San Diego, rebosante de vida, y el multifacético Parque de Mission Bay con su fascinante Sea World. En la parte costera del centro se halla el Museo Marítimo flotante y cerca la nueva y singular área de compras al lado de la bahía llamada Seaport Village. Atractivas comunidades de recreo también llenan las orillas del mar. Hay muy pocas personas que pueden pasar por alto la hermosura de La Jolla, la "Joya del Pacífico", o el ambiente isleño de Coronado.

Destacando el aspecto histórico, el Monumento Nacional de Cabrillo en el cabo de Punta Loma conmemora el descubrimiento de la costa de California hace unos cuatro siglos y medio por Juan Rodríguez Cabrillo. El Parque Histórico Estatal de Old Town (Pueblo Viejo) preserva el lugar de nacimiento de California y San Diego. En Old Town muchos de los edificios más viejos de California todavía se usan como restaurantes y tiendas, así como para museos.

Al sur de Old Town se halla el moderno centro, un escaparate siempre expansible de exposición de renovaciones atentas y diseño moderno.

Uno de los parques municipales más grandes del mundo se ubica junto al centro de San Diego. El lujuriante Parque de Balboa destaca excelentes museos, teatros y galerías con arquitectura sobresaliente reflejando el patrimonio español de la ciudad. Aquí se halla además el famoso Zoo de San Diego con su abundancia de plantas y animales exóticos. El Zoo también mantiene un gran santuario para animales salvajes al norte de la ciudad que se llama el Wild Animal Park de San Diego, en donde se puede observar a muchos animales andando libremente al igual que en su ambiente natural.

Viajando desde la costa hacia el este del condado por aldeas, pueblos y ciudades, pasando campos de flores commerciales, ranchos y huertos, por pintorescos valles productivos, pronto se llega a lo posterior del área metropolitana. Ahora se ve un mundo distinto con imponentes montañas, campos adornados con flores y fauna silvestres, lagos y ríos intermitentes. Mucho de esto es protegido por el vasto Bosque Nacional de Cleveland y varios Parques Estatales de California.

Con tantas ventajas disponibles, no es de extrañarse que el mundo sigue respondiendo a la fascinación de San Diego.

SAN DIEGO

サンデイエゴは人々を魅きつけてやみません。アメリカの主要な大都市の一つとして多くの訪問客を迎へているのは当然のことですが、サンデイエゴの場合は、同じ訪問客を何辺も繰返し呼び寄せる力を持っており、またその大部分の人々は望んで居住者になっております。

さて、そのサンデイエゴの魅力は一体何でしょうか？まず第一に挙げられるのは、地中海のそれに匹敵する素晴らしい気候であります。比較的低い湿度、少ない降雨量、高い快適指数および穏やかな年間平均気温(21℃)などに示されるように、気候の良さについては何人も疑いをはさみません。
次に海に親しむことが好きな人々にな、太平洋に面するサンデイエゴ郡の海岸線上の遊び場は数に限りがないように見えます。変化に富むその海岸線は四季を問わず釣り、遊泳、サーフイングおよびヨットのための理想的な場所を提供しています。

清潔で広々とした海辺や岩の多い入江もたくさんあります。さらに多くの生命を包容する美しいサンデイエゴ湾と、人気衰えぬシーワールドのあるミッション・ベイ公園があります。下町の海べりには、海上に浮かぶ海洋博物館があります。またそのそばにはシーポート・ヴィレッヂと呼ばれるユニークな海辺のショッピング・センターがあります。
美しい別荘地帯も海外線上に位置しています。"太平洋の宝石"と呼ばれる美しいラホヤや島の雰囲気を持つコロナドは大ていの人々にとって見逃すことはできないところです。

歴史的な観点からはロマ岬の先端にあるカブリーヨ国定記念碑は400〜450年前のJ．ロドリブス・カブリーヨのカリフオルニア海岸発見を記念したものです。またオールドタウン州立歴史公園にはそのカリフオルニアとサンデイエゴ発祥の地点が保存されています。
オールドタウンでは、カリフオルニア最古の建造物の多くがレストランや店輔としてあるいは博物館として現在も依然として使用されています。

オールドタウンの南側は近代的なビジネスの中心街です。たえまなく発展を続ける企画をこらした刷新性と近代的デザインのショーケースと表現してよいでしょう。
世界最大の市街公園の一つがサンデイエゴ下町に隣接してることもサンデイエゴの魅力の一つです。緑の影濃いバルボア公園の特徴はこの市のスペイン時代の遺産を象徴するすばらしい建築物とともに第一級の博物館、劇場、美術館を擁していることです。
また、ここには、珍種の植物や動物をその財産とする有名なサンデイエゴ動物園もあります。
この動物園はサンデイエゴ野性動物公園と呼ばれる一つの大きな野性動物保護区域も運営しています。　そこではたくさんの動物がその自然の環境の中で、気のおもむくままに自由に歩き廻っているのを観ることができます。

サンデイエゴ郡の海岸線から東に向って、村や町や市街を通り抜け、栽培用花畑、農場や果樹園を通り抜けさらには色彩に富んだ生産的な谷あいをいくつか通り抜けると間もなく都市地域の裏庭へ出ます。そこは、林立する山並み、野性の花に彩られた野原、湖、渓流および野性生物などのある別世界です。この地域の大部分は広大なクリーブランド国有林およびいくつかのカリフオルニア州立公園の一部を形成し保護されています。
皆さんも十分に納得ゆくまでサンデイエゴの門を叩いて下さい。そうすれば世界中がサンデイエゴの魅力を話題にし続けているという事実が何ら不思議ではなくなります。

SAN DIEGO

1　2　The San Diego Harbor
Le Port de San Diego
Der Hafen von San Diego
El Puerto de San Diego
サンデイエゴ港

2

3 4 Cabrillo National Monument on Point Loma
Monument National Cabrillo à la Pointe Loma
Das Cabrillo National Monument am Point Loma
El Monumento Nacional de Cabrillo en Point Loma
ロマ岬のカブリーヨ国定記念碑

3

5

6

San Diego sunset
San Diego au soleil couchant
Sonnenuntergang in San Diego
Puesta del sol en San Diego
サンデイエゴの夕日

7 8 Harbor lights
Les lumières du port
Der Hafen bei Nacht
Luces del puerto
港の灯

8

Strelitzia reginae

9 Star of India, a main attraction at the Maritime Museum
Star of India—Point d'intérêt au musée maritime
Der Stern von Indien, eine Hauptattraktion im Maritime Museum
"Star of India", una atracción principal del Museo Marítimo
客船"インドの星"：海洋博物館の中心展示物

10 San Diego Marriott Hotel and Marina
L'Hotel San Diego Marriott et son port
San Diego Marriott Hotel and Marina
El Hotel San Diego Marriott y Marina
サンディエゴ マリアット ホテル と マリナ

11

Dietes vegeta

12

11 12 Seaport Village: Specialty shops and restaurants in a unique waterfront setting
Seaport Village: Boutiques et restaurants donnant sur le port
Seaport Village: Geschäfte und Restaurants außergewöhnlich angelegt, direkt am Meer
Seaport Village: Tiendas de especialidades y restaurantes en una singular colocación portuaria
シーポート・ヴィレッヂ：ユニークな構成の水際に各種専門店およびレストランがひしめく。

14

13

15 San Diego Convention Center
San Diego, Convention Center
Le Centre de Conventions de San Diego
Das Convention Center in San Diego
サンディエゴ コンベンション センター

16 Federal complex
Bâtiments du Gouvernement Fédéral
Ministerien
Conjunto federal
連邦政府庁舎

17 The San Diego Trolley links downtown to the Mexican border
Le trolley relie San Diego du centre de la ville jusqu'à la frontière du Mexique
San Diegos Straßenbahn verbindet die Innenstadt mit der mexikanischen Grenze
El Tranvía de San Diego conecta el centro con la frontera mexicana
サンデイエゴ下町とメキシコ国境を結ぶトロリーバス

17

18

18 The Santa Fe Depot
Gare Santa Fe
Der Santa Fe Bahnhof
El Terminal del Santa Fe
サンタ フエ駅

19 20 Downtown's Horton Plaza
Horton Plaza en center-ville
Horton Plaza in der innenstadt
Centro comercial Horton Plaza
下町のホートンプラザ

21

21 22 23 24 Beautiful architecture housing galleries, museums, theaters and a botanical garden lines El Prado in Balboa Park

Architecture magnifique où se trouvent galeries, musées, théatres et un jardin botanique sur l'avenue El Prado qui borde le parc Balboa

Gallerien, Museen Theater und ein Botanischer Garten entlag der Straße "El Prado" im Bilboa Park, fallen durch besonders schöne Architektur ins Auge

Hermosa arquitectura encerrando galerías, museos, teatros y un jardín botánico a lo largo de El Prado en el Parque Balboa

バルボア公園の中のエルプラド通りにある美しい建造物。画廊、博物館、劇場および植物園がその中にある。

23

Echium fastuosum

Nymphaea sp

Protea sp.

24

25

Kniphofia sp.

26

Ficus sp.

25 26

The San Diego Zoo is home for thousands of exotic plants and animals

Le jardin zoologique où on y trouve en grand nombre des plantes exotiques et des animaux de toutes sortes

Der San Diego Zoo behiematet tausende von exotischen Pflanzen und Tieren

El Zoo de San Diego ampara miles de plantas y animales exóticos

サンデイエゴ動物園は数千種にのぼる珍しい植物や動物の住いとなっている。

Opuntia sp.

Opuntia sp.

Trichocereus

27

27 28 29 Old Town's Presidio Park and Serra Museum
Le parc Presidio et le Musée Serra dans le vieux quartier
Presidio Park und Serra Museum in der Altstadt
El Parque Presidio y Museo Serra de Old Town (Pueblo Viejo)
オールドタウンのプレシデイオ公園とセラ博物館。

28

31

30

30 31 32 Charming, historic Old Town
33 34 35 Le charme historique du vieux quartier
Old Town—die reizvolle historische Altstadt
El encantador e histórico Old Town
歴史を秘めて魅惑的なオールド・タウン

Tabebuia sp.

Hibiscus rosa-sinensis

33

32

34

35

Musa Paradisiaca

36 Old Town's Casa de Bandini is now a restaurant
Casa de Bandini est maintenant un restaurant du vieux quartier
Casa de Bandini in der Altstadt ist jetzt ein Restaurant
La Casa de Bandini de Old Town es ahora un restaurante
オールド・タウンのバンデイーニの家。現在はレストランとなっている。

Chrysanthemum frutescens

37 San Diego Jack Murphy Stadium
L'stade Jack Murphy
Das Kampfbahn Jack Murphy

Estadio Jack Murphy

サン・ディエゴ ジャック・マーフィー スタジアム

38

39

39 40 Rural San Diego County near Jamul
Vue champêtre du County de San Diego
Die ländliche Umgebung San Diegos bei Jamul
Lo rural del Condado de San Diego cerca de Jamul
サンデイエゴ郡のひなびた風景 ─ ジヤマル付近。

40

41 Water seeps from a rocky ledge near Guatay Mountain
L'eau qui s'échappe d'un rocher près du mont Guatay
Von einem Felsvorsprung in der Nähe des Guatay Berges sickert Wasser
Se rezuma agua de un saliente rocoso cerca del Monte Guatay
水が湧き出るグオーテイ山付近の岩

41

42

42 Cuyamaca Rancho State Park
Parc Cuyamaca Rancho
Cuyamaca Rancho State Park
El Parque Estatal de Rancho Cuyamaca
カイアマカ ランチョ 州立公園

43 Palomar Observatory high on Palomar Mountain
L'observatoire Palomar au haut de la montagne Palomar
Hoch oben auf dem Palomar Berg liegt das Palomar Observatorium
El Observatorio Palomar en las alturas del Monte Palomar
パロマー山頂のパロマー天文台

Ranunculus asiaticus

44

45

46

47

Protea sp.

48 49 50 The San Diego Wild Animal Park near Escondido
Parc destiné aux bêtes sauvages près de la ville d'Escondido
Der San Diego Wild Animal Park bei Escondido
El Wild Animal Park de San Diego cerca de Escondido
エスコンデイド付近のサンデイエゴ野性動物公園

48

49

50

51

51 52 Inviting La Jolla Cove in La Jolla

L'invitante petite baie La Jolla
La Jolla Cove (bahía) nos invita a La Jolla
La Jolla Cove in La Jolla lädt zum Besuch ein
人気を呼ぶサンデイエゴ郡ラ・ホヤの入り江

52

53 54 55 Romance is the mood as dusk settles on La Jolla's lovely shoreline
A la nuit tombante, on se donne à la rêverie et le beau rivage de La Jolla prend un air romantique
La Jolla liebliche Küstenlandschaft wirkt in der Abenddämmerung sehr romantisch
El ambiente romántico del crepúsculo en el bello borde de la playa de La Jolla
ラホヤの海岸線に夕やみが迫る頃、ロマンスのムードも最高潮

56 La Jolla is an educational and scientific center, with the University of California at San Diego, Scripps Institute of Oceanography and the Salk Institute based here. Pictured is the UCSD library.

La Jolla est un centre éducationel et scientifique. L'Université de Californie de San Diego se trouve là, l'institut d'océanographie, Scripps et l'institut Salk y sont aussi. On voit ici la bibliothèque de l'Université de Californie de San Diego, UCSD.

La Jolla gilt als Zentrum für Bildung und Wissenschaft. Der San Diego Campus der Universität von Kalifornien, das Scripps Institut für Ozeanographie und das Salk Institut sind hier zu Hause. Auf dem Bild sieht man die Bibliothek der Universität.

La Jolla es un centro educacional y científico, hallándose aquí las centrales de la Universidad de California en San Diego, del Instituto de Oceanografía Scripps y del Instituto Salk. En la foto se ve la biblioteca de la UCSD.

ラホヤは教育および科学の中心地である。カリフォルニア大学サンデイエゴ校、海洋学のスクリップ研究所およびソーク研究所の存在が それを象徴している。

Coreopsis maritima

57 Rare Torrey Pines are protected at Torrey Pines State Reserve **57**
Le pins Torrey, très rares, son protégés par le gouvernement dans une réserve à ce but
Die seltene Torrey Tanne steht im Torrey Pines State Reservat unter Naturschutz
Raros Pinos de Torrey hallan protección en la Reserva Estatal de Torrey Pines
稀らしいトーレイパインの群落が州立のトーレイパイン保護区域に保護されている。

58 Behind a breaker
Derrière les brisants
Hinter einer Woge
Detrás de una oleada
防波堤の後景

59 The ever popular Pacific Beach
La fameuse plage Pacific Beach toujours attirante
Pacific Beach—ein allgemein beliebter Strand
La siempre popular playa de Pacific Beach
歴史的に有名な太平洋に面した海岸

60 60 61 Mission Bay Park, devoted to water sports and recreation
Le parc Mission Bay où l'on s'adonne aux sports nautiques de toutes sortes
Mission Bay Park—dem Wassersport und der Erholung gewidmet
El Parque de Mission Bay, dedicado a deportes acuáticos y al recreo
ミッション・ベイ公園 — 水上スポーツおよびレクレーションの中心

61

62 Sea World, a marine life center is located in Mission Bay Park **62**

Sea World, un centre de vie aquatique à Mission Bay Park

Sea World, ein Zentrum für Meereskunde, liegt im Mission Bay Park

Sea World, un centro de vida marina, se sitúa en el Parque de Mission Bay

海洋生物センターとしてのシー・ワールドはミッションベイ水生動物公園の中にある。

64 The Hotel Del Coronado, a Victorian masterpiece and national historic landmark

L'Hôtel Del Coronado, un chef-d'oeuvre d'architecture du style victorien, fait maintenant partie des bâtiments officiellement désignés par la société historique comme étant un point d'intérêt national

Das Coronado Hotel, ein Meisterwerk der viktorianischen Epoche, steht unter nationalem Denkmalschutz

El Hotel del Coronado, obra maestra victoriana y marca nacional histórica

デル・コロナド・ホテル—ヴィクトリア朝風建築の傑作で国定歴史建造物に指定されている。

63 California's Mission chain began with the Mission San Diego de Alcala

L'enchaînement des missions en Californie commença avec la Mission San Diego de Alcala

Die Mission San Diego de Alcala, die erste in Kaliforniens Missionskette

La cadena de misiones de California comenzó con la Misión de San Diego de Alcalá

カリフォルニア・ミッション寺院チエインはアルカラのサンデイエゴミッション寺院を起点とする。

65 66 San Diego-Coronado Bay Bridge
Le pont reliant San Diego et la baie Coronado
Die San Diego-Coronado Bay Brücke
El Puente de San Diego y la Bahía de Coronado
サンデイエゴーコロナド間を結ぶ港湾橋

67 Coronado sunset
Coronado au soleil couchant
Sonnenuntergang in Coronado
Puesta del sol en Coronado
コロナド島の夕日

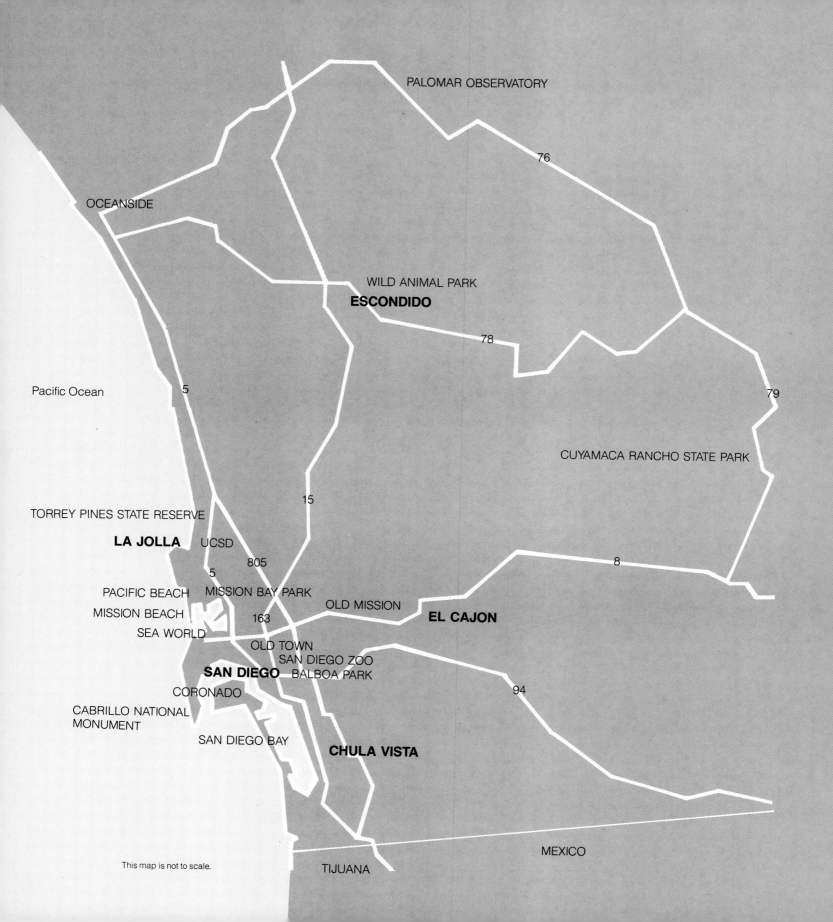

PALOMAR OBSERVATORY

OCEANSIDE

76

WILD ANIMAL PARK

ESCONDIDO

Pacific Ocean

5

78

79

CUYAMACA RANCHO STATE PARK

TORREY PINES STATE RESERVE

LA JOLLA   UCSD

805

15

5

PACIFIC BEACH

MISSION BAY PARK

8

MISSION BEACH

163

OLD MISSION

EL CAJON

SEA WORLD

OLD TOWN

SAN DIEGO ZOO

SAN DIEGO   BALBOA PARK

CORONADO

94

CABRILLO NATIONAL
MONUMENT

SAN DIEGO BAY

CHULA VISTA

This map is not to scale.

MEXICO

TIJUANA

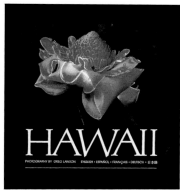

HAWAII

Photography by Greg Lawson. The wondrous beauty of the Hawaiian Islands captured for you on Hawaii, Kauai, Lanai, Maui, Molokai and Oahu. Introduction and captions in English, Spanish, French, German and Japanese. ISBN 0-96068-4-7-5

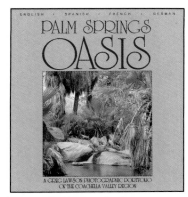

PALM SPRINGS OASIS

An elegant display of beautiful Palm Springs and the Coachella Valley. Showcases breathtaking sights at every elevation, from enchanting spring-fed canyons to brilliant desert flowers. Introduction and captions in English, Spanish, French and German. ISBN 0-916251-40-3

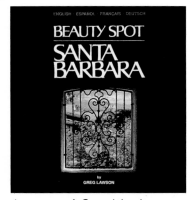

BEAUTY SPOT SANTA BARBARA

Photography by Greg Lawson. A Spanish city on the California coast is revealed in this photographic tour of lovely Santa Barbara. Includes the Santa Ynez Valley. Introduction and captions in English, Spanish, French and German. ISBN 0-9606704-1-6

CALIFORNIA

Photography by Ralph Cernuda and Greg Lawson. A potpourri of "The Golden State" from the High Sierra to the restless sea. Includes selected cities, national parks and monuments and much more. Introduction and captions in English, Spanish, French, German and Japanese. ISBN 0-916251-33-0

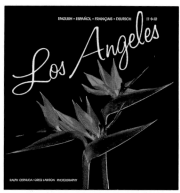

LOS ANGELES

Photography by Ralph Cernuda and Greg Lawson. A new look at the great city. Covers the Los Angeles area from Santa Monica to the San Bernardino Mountains, from Ventura to Orange Counties. Introduction and captions in English, Spanish, French, German and Japanese. ISBN 0-9606704-9-1

I welcome you to travel with Greg Lawson through awe-inspiring photographic journeys in these superb pictorial publications. See how each title captures the uniqueness and natural ambience of its region. For a complimentary catalog featuring our line of soft cover and large format titles, please write to: P.O. Box 21291, El Cajon, CA 92021.

My Best To You

Mark D. Rasche
Publisher